Keto Diet for Vegetarians

Easy Low-Carb Recipes
to Lose Weight
and Strengthen your Body

Ricardo Abagnale

0

Table of Contents

3

INTRODUCTION

The Ketogenic diet is truly life changing. The diet improves your overall health and helps you lose the extra weight in a matter of days. The diet will show its multiple benefits even from the beginning and it will become your new lifestyle really soon.

As soon as you embrace the Ketogenic diet, you will start to live a completely new life.

On the other hand, the vegetarian diet is such a healthy dietary option you can choose when trying to live healthy and also lose some weight.

The collection we bring to you today is actually a combination between the Ketogenic and vegetarian diets. You get to discover some amazing Ketogenic vegetarian dishes you can prepare in the comfort of your own home. All the dishes you found here follow both the Ketogenic and the vegetarian rules, they all taste delicious and rich and they are all easy to make.

We can assure you that such a combo is hard to find. So, start a keto diet with a vegetarian "touch" today. It will be both useful and fun!

So, what are you still waiting for? Get started with the Ketogenic diet and learn how to prepare the best and most flavored Ketogenic vegetarian dishes. Enjoy them all!

Avocado Spinach Cucumber Breakfast Smoothie

Preparation time: 10 minutes

Servings: 1

Nutritional Values (Per Serving):
- Calories: 385
- Fat: 26.6 g
- Carbohydrates: 12.9 g
- Sugar: 2.7 g

- Protein: 26.1 g
- Cholesterol: 65 mg

Ingredients:

- 1 scoop protein powder
- 1 ½ cups almond milk
- 1-ounce spinach, fresh, chopped
- 1.8-ounces cucumber, chopped
- 1.8-ounce celery, chopped
- 1.8-ounce avocado
- 1 tablespoon coconut oil
- 10 drops liquid Stevia

Directions:

1. Add all the ingredients into a blender and blend until smooth. Serve and enjoy!

Keto Flax Cinnamon Muffins

Preparation time: 10 minutes

Cooking time: 20 minutes

Servings: 12

Nutritional Values (Per Serving):

- Calories: 219
- Fat: 20 g
- Carbohydrates: 6 g
- Sugar: 1 g
- Protein: 6 g
- Cholesterol: 55 mg

Ingredients:

- 5 organic eggs, beaten
- 1/8 teaspoon salt
- 1 cup flax seed, ground
- ½ cup olive oil
- ½ cup coconut sugar
- ¼ cup coconut flour
- 2 teaspoons vanilla
- 2 teaspoons cinnamon

- 1 teaspoon lemon juice
- ½ teaspoon baking soda
- 1 cup walnuts, chopped

Directions:

1. Preheat your oven to 350°Fahrenheit. Spray muffin pan with cooking spray and set aside.
2. Add all ingredients into a mixing bowl and mix well to combine. Pour the batter into prepared muffin pan— filling each about ¾ full of mixture.
3. Bake for about 20 minutes.
4. Serve and enjoy!

Parsley Chard Salad

Preparation time: 10 minutes

Cooking time: 0 minutes

Servings: 4

Nutritional Values (Per Serving):

- calories 250
- fat 4
- fiber 8
- carbs 20
- protein 6.5

Ingredients:

- 1 pound red chard, steamed and torn
- 1 cup grapes, halved
- 1 cup cherry tomatoes, halved

- 1 celery stalk, chopped

- 3 tablespoons balsamic vinegar

- ½ cup coconut cream

- 1 teaspoon chili powder

- 2 tablespoons olive oil

- ½ cup parsley, minced

- A pinch of sea salt and black pepper

Directions:

1. In a bowl, combine the chard with the grapes, tomatoes and the other ingredients, toss and serve right away.

Bok Choy Salad

Preparation time: 10 minutes

Cooking time: 20 minutes

Servings: 4

Nutritional Values (Per Serving):

- Calories 107
- Fat 8.4
- Fiber 3.4
- Carbs 9
- Protein 3.1

Ingredients:

- 4 scallions, chopped
- 1 pound bok choy, torn
- 2 tablespoons olive oil
- ½ cup veggie stock
- 2 tablespoons balsamic vinegar
- 1 tablespoon chili powder
- 1 cup cherry tomatoes, halved
- 1 tablespoon garlic powder
- ¼ cup chives, chopped
- 1 teaspoon rosemary, dried
- 1 tablespoon thyme, chopped
- A pinch of sea salt and black pepper

Directions:

1. Heat up a pan with the oil over medium heat, add the scallions, garlic powder and rosemary, stir and cook for 5 minutes.
2. Add the bok choy and the rest of the ingredients, toss, cook over medium heat for 15 minutes, divide between plates and serve.

Roasted Bok Choy and Sprouts Mix

Preparation time: 10 minutes

Cooking time: 30 minutes

Servings: 4

Nutritional Values (Per Serving):

- Calories 100
- Fat 2
- Fiber 2
- Carbs 9
- Protein 1

Ingredients:

- 2 tablespoons olive oil
- 1 pound Brussels sprouts, trimmed and halved
- ½ pound bok choy, torn

- 1 tablespoon garlic powder
- 1 tablespoon chili powder
- 2 tablespoons balsamic vinegar
- 1 tablespoon onion powder
- A pinch of salt and black pepper
- 1 teaspoon sweet paprika

Directions:

1. In a roasting pan, combine the bok choy with the sprouts, the oil and the other ingredients, toss and cook at 390 degrees F for 30 minutes.
2. Divide the mix between plates and serve right away.

Bok Choy and Cauliflower Rice

Preparation time: 10 minutes

Cooking time: 20 minutes

Servings: 4

Nutritional Values (Per Serving):

- Calories 130
- Fat 2
- Fiber 2
- Carbs 6
- Protein 8

Ingredients:

- 2 tablespoons olive oil
- 2 garlic cloves, minced
- 4 scallions, chopped
- 2 cups cauliflower rice
- 1 cup bok choy, torn

- ½ cup cherry tomatoes, halved
- 2 tablespoons thyme, chopped
- 1 tablespoon lemon juice
- Zest of ½ lemon, grated
- A pinch of sea salt and black pepper

Directions:

1. Heat up a pan with the oil over medium heat, add the scallions and the garlic and sauté for 5 minutes.
2. Add the cauliflower rice and the other ingredients, toss, cook over medium heat for 15 minutes more, divide into bowls and serve.

Sweet Kale and Onions Mix

Preparation time: 10 minutes

Cooking time: 12 minutes

Servings: 4

Nutritional Values (Per Serving):

- Calories 150
- Fat 4
- Fiber 4
- Carbs 8.2
- Protein 5

Ingredients:

- 4 cups kale, torn
- 4 spring onions, chopped
- ½ cup tomato passata
- 1 teaspoon stevia
- 2 tablespoons avocado oil

- A pinch of sea salt and black pepper
- 1 teaspoon sweet paprika

Directions:

1. Heat up a pan with the oil over medium high heat, add the spring onions, paprika and stevia, toss and cook for 2 minutes.
2. Add the kale and the other ingredients, toss, cook over medium heat for 10 minutes, divide between plates and serve right away.

Broccoli, Chard and Kale Mix

Preparation time: 10 minutes

Cooking time: 20 minutes

Servings: 4

Nutritional Values (Per Serving):

- Calories 90
- Fat 1
- Fiber 3
- Carbs 7
- Protein 2

Ingredients:

- ½ cup kale, torn
- 2 cups red chard, torn
- 2 cups broccoli florets
- 4 garlic cloves, minced
- 2 tablespoons olive oil

- 1 tablespoon balsamic vinegar
- 1 tablespoon lemon juice
- ½ cup almonds, sliced
- 1 tablespoon chives, chopped

Directions:

1. In a roasting pan, combine the kale with the chard, broccoli and the other ingredients, toss and bake at 400 degrees F for 20 minutes.
2. Divide everything between plates and serve right away.

Baked Bok Choy and Tomatoes

Preparation time: 10 minutes

Cooking time: 30 minutes

Servings: 4

Nutritional Values (Per Serving):

- Calories 220
- Fat 2
- Fiber 4
- Carbs 6
- Protein 10

Ingredients:

- 1 pound bok choy, torn
- ½ pound cherry tomatoes, halved
- 2 tablespoons olive oil
- 2 teaspoons rosemary, dried
- ½ teaspoon nutmeg, ground

- 1 teaspoon cloves, ground
- 1 teaspoon coriander, ground
- 2 tablespoons balsamic vinegar

Directions:

1. In a roasting pan, combine the bok choy with the cherry tomatoes and the other ingredients, toss and bake at 400 degrees F for 30 minutes,
2. Divide everything between plates and serve.

Italian Bok Choy, Rice and Arugula Salad

Preparation time: 10 minutes

Cooking time: 0 minutes

Servings: 4

Nutritional Values (Per Serving):

- Calories 227
- Fat 2
- Fiber 7
- Carbs 18
- Protein 11

Ingredients:

- 2 cups cauliflower rice, steamed
- 1 cup bok choy, torn
- ½ cup baby arugula

- 2 tablespoons pine nuts, toasted
- 1 tablespoon walnuts, chopped
- 2 tomatoes, cubed
- 2 tablespoons avocado oil
- 2 garlic cloves, minced
- 2 tablespoons basil, chopped
- 1 tablespoon Italian seasoning
- 2 tablespoons lime juice
- A pinch of sea salt and black pepper

Directions:

1. In a salad bowl, combine the cauliflower rice with the arugula, bok choy and the other ingredients, toss, divide into smaller bowls and serve.

Hot Cranberries and Arugula Mix

Preparation time: 10 minutes

Cooking time: 0 minutes

Servings: 4

Nutritional Values (Per Serving):

- Calories 110
- Fat 4
- Fiber 2

- Carbs 10
- Protein 2

Ingredients:

- 1 cup cranberries
- 2 cups baby arugula
- 1 avocado, peeled, pitted and cubed
- 1 cucumber, cubed
- ¼ cup kalamata olives, pitted and sliced
- 1 tablespoon walnuts, chopped
- 2 tablespoons olive oil
- 2 tablespoons lime juice

Directions:

1. In a bowl, combine the arugula with the cranberries and the other ingredients, toss well, divide between plates and serve.

Cauliflower Salad

Preparation time: 10 minutes

Cooking time: 0 minutes

Servings: 4

Nutritional Values (Per Serving):

- Calories 211
- Fat 20
- Fiber 2
- Carbs 3
- Protein 4

Ingredients:

- 1 pound cauliflower florets, blanched
- 1 avocado, peeled, pitted and cubed
- 1 cup kalamata olives, pitted and halved

- Salt and black pepper to the taste
- 1 cup spring onions, chopped
- 1 tablespoon lime juice
- 1 tablespoon chives, chopped

Directions:

1. In a bowl, combine the cauliflower florets with the avocado and the other ingredients, toss and serve as a side salad.

Turmeric Carrots

Preparation time: 10 minutes

Cooking time: 40 minutes

Servings: 4

Nutritional Values (Per Serving):

- Calories 79
- Fat 3.8
- Fiber 3.7
- Carbs 10.9
- Protein 1

Ingredients:

- 1 pound baby carrots, peeled
- 1 tablespoon olive oil
- 2 spring onions, chopped
- 2 tablespoons balsamic vinegar
- 2 garlic cloves, minced

- 1 teaspoon turmeric powder

- 1 tablespoon chives, chopped

- ¼ teaspoon cayenne pepper

- A pinch of salt and black pepper

Directions:

1. Spread the carrots on a baking sheet lined with parchment paper, add the oil, the spring onions and the other ingredients, toss and bake at 380 degrees F for 40 minutes.
2. Divide the carrots between plates and serve.

Spinach Mix

Preparation time: 10 minutes

Cooking time: 12 minutes

Servings: 4

Nutritional Values (Per Serving):

- Calories 71
- Fat 4
- Fiber 3.2
- Carbs 7.4
- Protein 3.7

Ingredients:

- 1 pound baby spinach
- 1 yellow onion, chopped
- 1 tablespoon olive oil
- 1 tablespoon lemon juice
- 2 garlic cloves, minced

- A pinch of cayenne pepper
- ¼ teaspoon smoked paprika
- A pinch of salt and black pepper

Directions:

1. Heat up a pan with the oil over medium-high heat, add the onion and the garlic and sauté for 2 minutes.
2. Add the spinach and the other ingredients, toss, cook over medium heat for 10 minutes, divide between plates and serve as a side dish.

Orange Carrots

Preparation time: 5 minutes

Cooking time: 25 minutes

Servings: 4

Nutritional Values (Per Serving):

- Calories 140
- Fat 3.9
- Fiber 5
- Carbs 26.1
- Protein 2.1

Ingredients:

- 1 pound carrots, peeled and roughly sliced
- 1 yellow onion, chopped
- 1 tablespoon olive oil
- Zest of 1 orange, grated
- Juice of 1 orange
- 1 orange, peeled and cut into segments
- 1 tablespoon rosemary, chopped

Directions:

1. Heat up a pan with the oil over medium-high heat, add the onion and sauté for 5 minutes.
2. Add the carrots, the orange zest and the other ingredients, toss, cook over medium heat for 20 minutes more, divide between plates and serve.

Endive Sauté

Preparation time: 5 minutes

Cooking time: 15 minutes

Servings: 4

Nutritional Values (Per Serving):

- Calories 110
- Fat 4.4
- Fiber 12.8
- Carbs 16.2
- Protein 5.6

Ingredients:

- 3 endives, shredded
- 1 tablespoon olive oil
- 4 scallions, chopped
- ½ cup tomato sauce
- 2 garlic cloves, minced

- A pinch of sea salt and black pepper
- 1/8 teaspoon turmeric powder
- 1 tablespoon chives, chopped

Directions:

1. Heat up a pan with the oil over medium heat, add the scallions and the garlic and sauté for 5 minutes.
2. Add the endives and the other ingredients, toss, cook everything for 10 minutes more, divide between plates and serve as a side dish.

Zucchini Pan

Preparation time: 5 minutes

Cooking time: 20 minutes

Servings: 4

Nutritional Values (Per Serving):

- Calories 170
- Fat 5
- Fiber 2
- Carbs 11
- Protein 7

Ingredients:

- 1 pound zucchinis, sliced
- 1 yellow onion, chopped
- 2 tablespoons olive oil
- 2 apples, peeled, cored and cubed
- 1 tomato, cubed

- 1 tablespoon rosemary, chopped
- 1 tablespoon chives, chopped

Directions:

1. Heat up a pan with the oil over medium heat, add the onion and sauté for 5 minutes.
2. Add the zucchinis and the other ingredients, toss, cook over medium heat for 15 minutes more, divide between plates and serve as a side dish.

Cardamom Carrots with Orange

Preparation time: 5 minutes

Cooking time: 10 minutes

Servings: 4

Ingredients:

- 1 pound carrots, cut into 1/4-inch slices
- 2 tablespoons vegan margarine
- 1 tablespoon finely grated orange zest
- 1/2 teaspoon ground cardamom
- Salt
- Ground cayenne

Directions:

1. Steam the carrots until tender, about 7 minutes. Set aside.

2. In a large skillet, melt the margarine over medium heat. Add the carrots, orange zest, and cardamom and season with salt and cayenne to taste. Cook, stirring occasionally, until flavors are blended, about 2 minutes. Serve immediately

Stuffed Baby Peppers

Preparation time: 10 minutes

Cooking time: 0 minutes

Servings: 4

Nutritional Values (Per Serving):

- Calories 371
- Fat 14
- Fiber 3,2
- Carbs 20,9
- Protein 30,5

Ingredients:

- 12 baby bell peppers, cut into halves lengthwise and seeds removed
- ¼ teaspoon red pepper flakes, crushed
- 1 pound shrimp, cooked, peeled and deveined
- 6 tablespoons jarred Paleo pesto
- A pinch of sea salt

- Black pepper to taste
- 1 tablespoon lemon juice
- 1 tablespoon olive oil
- A handful parsley, chopped

Directions:

1. In a bowl, mix shrimp with pepper flakes, Paleo pesto, a pinch of salt, black pepper, lemon juice, oil and parsley and whisk well.
2. Divide this into bell pepper halves, arrange on plates and serve.
3. Enjoy!

Baked Eggplant

Preparation time: 10 minutes

Cooking time: 30 minutes

Servings: 3

Nutritional Values (Per Serving):

- Calories 303
- Fat 19,6
- Fiber 16,9
- Carbs 28,6
- Protein 10,3

Ingredients:

- 2 eggplants, sliced
- A pinch of sea salt
- Black pepper to taste
- 1 cup almonds, ground

- 1 teaspoon garlic, minced
- 2 teaspoons olive oil

Directions:

1. Grease a baking dish with some of the oil and arrange eggplant slices on it.
2. Season them with a pinch of salt and some black pepper and leave them aside for 10 minutes.
3. In a food processor, mix almonds with the rest of the oil, garlic, a pinch of salt and black pepper and blend well.
4. Spread this over eggplant slices, place in the oven at 425 degrees F and bake for 30 minutes.
5. Divide between plates and serve.
6. Enjoy!

Eggplant Mix

Preparation time: 10 minutes

Cooking time: 40 minutes

Servings: 3

Nutritional Values (Per Serving):

- Calories 533
- Fat 35,6
- Fiber 32,6
- Carbs 56,5
- Protein 9,4

Ingredients:

- 5 medium eggplants, sliced into rounds
- 1 teaspoon thyme, chopped
- 2 tablespoons balsamic vinegar
- 1 teaspoon mustard
- 2 garlic cloves, minced

- ½ cup olive oil Black pepper to taste
- A pinch of sea salt
- 1 teaspoon maple syrup

Directions:

1. In a bowl, mix vinegar with thyme, mustard, garlic, oil, salt, pepper and maple syrup and whisk very well.
2. Arrange eggplant round on a lined baking sheet, place in the oven at 425 degrees F and roast for 40 minutes.
3. Divide eggplants between plates and serve.
4. Enjoy!

Eggplant and Garlic Sauce

Preparation time: 10 minutes

Cooking time: 10 minutes

Servings: 4

Nutritional Values (Per Serving):

- Calories 123
- Fat 1,7
- Fiber 15,2
- Carbs 26,7
- Protein 4,4

Ingredients:

- 2 tablespoons avocado oil
- 2 garlic cloves, minced
- 3 eggplants, cut into halves and thinly sliced
- 1 red chili pepper, chopped
- 1 green onion stalk, chopped
- 1 tablespoon ginger, grated

- 1 tablespoon coconut aminos
- 1 tablespoon balsamic vinegar

Directions:

1. Heat up a pan with half of the oil over medium-high heat, add eggplant slices, cook for 2 minutes, flip, cook for 3 minutes more and transfer to a plate.
2. Heat up the pan with the rest of the oil over medium heat, add chili pepper, garlic, green onions and ginger, stir and cook for 1 minute.
3. Return eggplant slices to the pan, stir and cook for 1 minute.
4. Add coconut aminos and vinegar, stir, divide between plates and serve.
5. Enjoy!

Thai-Inspired Coconut Soup

Preparation time: 5 minutes

Cooking time: 25 minutes

Servings: 4

Ingredients:

- 1 tablespoon canola or grapeseed oil
- 1 medium onion, chopped
- 2 tablespoons minced fresh ginger
- 2 tablespoons soy sauce
- 1 tablespoon light brown sugar (optional)
- 1 teaspoon Asian chili paste
- 2½ cups light vegetable broth (homemade, store-bought, or water)
- 8 ounces extra-firm tofu, drained and cut into ½-inch dice
- 2 (13.5-ouncecans unsweetened coconut milk

- 1 tablespoon fresh lime juice
- 3 tablespoons chopped fresh cilantro, for garnish

Directions:

1. In a large soup pot, heat the oil over medium heat. Add the onion and ginger and cook until softened, about 5 minutes. Stir in the soy sauce, sugar, and chile paste. Add the broth and bring to a boil. Reduce heat to medium and simmer for 15 minutes.
2. Strain the broth and discard solids. Return the broth to the pot over medium heat. Add the tofu and stir in the coconut milk and lime juice. Simmer 5 minutes longer to allow flavors to blend.
3. Ladle into bowls, sprinkle with cilantro, and serve.

Curried Butternut and Red Lentil Soup with Chard

Preparation time: 5 minutes

Cooking time: 55 minutes

Servings: 4

Ingredients:

- 1 tablespoon olive oil
- 1 medium onion, chopped
- 1 medium butternut squash, peeled and diced
- 1 garlic clove, minced
- 1 tablespoon minced fresh ginger
- 1 tablespoon hot or mild curry powder
- 1 14.5-ouncecan crushed tomatoes
- 1 cup red lentils, picked over, rinsed, and drained
- 5 cups vegetable broth (homemade, store-bought, or water)
- Salt and freshly ground black pepper
- 3 cups chopped stemmed Swiss chard

Directions:

1. In a large soup pot, heat the oil over medium heat. Add the onion, squash, and garlic. Cover and cook until softened, about 10 minutes.

2. Stir in the ginger and curry powder, then add the tomatoes, lentils, broth, and salt and pepper to taste. Bring to boil, then reduce heat to low and simmer, uncovered, until the lentils and vegetables are tender, stirring occasionally, about 45 minutes.

3. About 15 minutes before serving, stir in the chard. Taste, adjusting seasonings if necessary, and serve.

Butternut Soup with a Swirl of Cranberry

Preparation time: 10 minutes

Cooking time: 30 minutes

Servings: 4 to 6

Ingredients:

- 2 tablespoons olive oil
- 1 medium onion, chopped
- 1 medium carrot, chopped
- 1/2 teaspoon ground allspice
- 1/4 teaspoon ground ginger
- 1 medium russet potato, peeled and chopped
- 3 pounds butternut squash, peeled, seeded, and cut into 1-inch pieces
- 4 cups vegetable broth (homemade, store-bought or water)
- Salt

- ½ cup whole berry cranberry sauce, homemade or canned
- 2 tablespoons fresh orange juice

Directions:

1. In a large soup pot, heat the oil over medium heat. Add the onion and carrot, cover, and cook, stirring occasionally, until softened, about 5 minutes. Stir in the allspice, ginger, potato, squash, broth, and salt to taste. Simmer, uncovered, until the vegetables are very soft, about 30 minutes.
2. While the soup is cooking, puree the cranberry sauce and orange juice in a blender or food processor. Run the pureed cranberry sauce through a strainer and discard solids. Set aside.
3. When the soup is done cooking, puree it in the pot with an immersion blender or in a blender or food processor, in batches if necessary, and return to the pot. Reheat the soup and taste, adjusting seasonings if necessary. Ladle into bowls, swirl a tablespoon or so of the reserved cranberry puree into the center of each bowl, and serve.

Spinach, Walnut, And Apple Soup

Preparation time: 10 minutes

Cooking time: 20 minutes

Servings: 4

Ingredients:

- 1 tablespoon olive oil
- 1 small onion, chopped

- 3 cups vegetable broth (homemad, store-bought or water)
- 2 Fuji or other flavorful apples
- 1 cup apple juice
- 4 cups fresh spinach
- ¾ cup ground walnuts
- 1 teaspoon minced fresh sage or ½ teaspoon dried
- ¼ teaspoon ground allspice
- Salt and freshly ground black pepper
- 1 cup soy milk
- ¼ cup toasted walnut pieces

Directions:

1. In a large soup pot, heat the oil over medium heat. Add the onion, cover, and cook until softened, 5 minutes. Add about 1 cup of the vegetable broth, cover, and cook until the onion is very soft, about 5 minutes longer.
2. Peel, core, and chop one of the apples and add it to the pot with the onion and broth. Add the apple juice, spinach, ground walnuts, sage, allspice, the remaining 2 cups broth, and salt and pepper to taste. Bring to a boil, then reduce heat to low and simmer for 10 minutes.

3. Puree the soup in the pot with an immersion blender or in a blender or food processor, in batches if necessary, and return to the pot. Stir in the soy milk and reheat over medium heat until hot.

4. Chop the remaining apple. Ladle the soup into bowls, garnish each bowl with some of the chopped apple, sprinkle with the walnut pieces, and serve.

Creamy Seitan Shirataki Fettucine

Preparation time: 35 minutes

Serving: 4

Nutritional Values (Per Serving):

- Calories: 720
- Total Fat: 56.5g
- Saturated Fat: 27.2g
- Total Carbs: 17 g
- Dietary Fiber:3g
- Sugar: 7g
- Protein: 37g
- Sodium:1764 mg

Ingredients:

For the shirataki fettuccine:

- 2 (8 oz) packs shirataki fettuccine

For the creamy seitan sauce:

- 5 tbsp butter
- 4 seitan slabs, cut into 2-inch cubes
- Salt and black pepper to taste
- 3 garlic cloves, minced
- 1 ¼ cups coconut cream
- ½ cup dry white wine
- 1 tsp grated lemon zest
- 1 cup baby spinach
- Lemon wedges for garnishing

Directions:

For the shirataki fettuccine:

1. Boil 2 cups of water in a medium pot over medium heat.
2. Strain the shirataki pasta through a colander and rinse very well under hot running water.

3. Allow proper draining and pour the shirataki pasta into the boiling water. Cook for 3 minutes and strain again.
4. Place a dry skillet over medium heat and stir-fry the shirataki pasta until visibly dry, and makes a squeaky sound when stirred, 1 to 2 minutes. Take off the heat and set aside.

For the seitan sauce:

5. Melt half of the butter in a large skillet; season the seitan with salt, black pepper, and cook in the butter until golden brown on all sides and flaky within, 8 minutes. Transfer to a plate and set aside.
6. Add the remaining butter to the skillet to melt and stir in the garlic. Cook until fragrant, 1 minute.
7. Mix in the coconut cream, white wine, lemon zest, salt, and black pepper. Allow boiling over low heat until the sauce thickens, 5 minutes.
8. Stir in the spinach, allow wilting for 2 minutes and stir in the shirataki fettuccine and seitan until well- coated in the sauce. Adjust the taste with salt and black pepper.
9. Dish the food and garnish with the lemon wedges. Serve warm.

Cucumber-Radish Salad with Tarragon Vinaigrette

Preparation time: 15 minutes

Cooking time: 0 minutes

Servings: 4

Ingredients:

- medium English cucumbers, peeled, halved, seeded, cut into 1/4-inch slices
- 6 small red radishes, cut into 1/8-inch slices
- 2 1/2 tablespoons tarragon vinegar
- 1/2 teaspoon dried tarragon
- 1/4 teaspoon sugar
- Salt and freshly ground black pepper
- 1/4 cup olive oil

Directions:

1. In a large bowl, combine the cucumbers and the radishes and set aside.

2. In a small bowl, combine the vinegar, tarragon, sugar, and salt and pepper to taste. Whisk in the oil until well blended, then add the dressing to the salad. Toss gently to combine and serve.

Italian-Style Pasta Salad

Preparation time: 5 minutes

Cooking time: 10 minutes

Servings: 4 to 6

Ingredients:

- 8 ounces penne, rotini, or other small pasta
- 1½ cups cooked or 1 (15.5-ouncecan chickpeas, drained and rinsed
- ½ cup pitted kalamata olives
- ½ cup minced oil-packed sun-dried tomatoes
- 1 (6-ouncejar marinated artichoke hearts, drained
- jarred roasted red peppers, chopped
- ½ cup frozen peas, thawed
- 1 tablespoon capers
- teaspoons dried chives
- ½ cup olive oil
- ¼ cup white wine vinegar
- ½ teaspoon dried basil

- 1 garlic clove, minced
- Salt and freshly ground black pepper

Directions:

1. In a pot of boiling salted water, cook the pasta, stirring occasionally, until al dente, about 10 minutes. Drain well and transfer to a large bowl. Add the chickpeas, olives, tomatoes, artichoke hearts, roasted peppers, peas, capers, and chives. Toss gently and set aside.
2. In a small bowl, combine the oil, vinegar, basil, garlic, sugar, and salt and black pepper to taste. Pour the dressing onto the pasta salad and toss to combine. Serve chilled or at room temperature.

Tabbouleh Salad

Preparation time: 15 minutes

Cooking time: 10 minutes

Servings: 4

Nutrition:

- Calories: 304
- Total fat: 11g
- Carbs: 44g
- Fiber: 6g
- Protein: 10g

Ingredients:

- 1 cup whole-wheat couscous
- 1 cup boiling water
- Zest and juice of 1 lemon
- 1 garlic clove, pressed
- Pinch sea salt

- 1 tablespoon olive oil, or flaxseed oil (optional)
- ½ cucumber, diced small
- 1 tomato, diced small
- 1 cup fresh parsley, chopped
- ¼ cup fresh mint, finely chopped
- 2 scallions, finely chopped
- tablespoons sunflower seeds (optional)

Directions:

1. Put the couscous in a medium bowl, and cover with boiling water until all the grains are submerged. Cover the bowl with a plate or wrap. Set aside.
2. Put the lemon zest and juice in a large salad bowl, then stir in the garlic, salt, and the olive oil (if using).
3. Put the cucumber, tomato, parsley, mint, and scallions in the bowl, and toss them to coat with the dressing. Take the plate off the couscous and fluff with a fork.
4. Add the cooked couscous to the vegetables, and toss to combine.
5. Serve topped with the sunflower seeds (if using).

Tuscan White Bean Salad

Preparation time: 10 minutes • marinating time: 30 minutes

Servings: 2

Nutrition:

- Calories: 360
- Total fat: 8g
- Carbs: 68g
- Fiber: 15g
- Protein: 18g

Ingredients:

For the dressing

- 1 tablespoon olive oil
- 2 tablespoons balsamic vinegar
- 1 teaspoon minced fresh chives, or scallions
- 1 garlic clove, pressed or minced
- 1 tablespoon fresh rosemary, chopped, or 1 teaspoon dried
- 1 tablespoon fresh oregano, chopped, or 1 teaspoon dried
- Pinch sea salt

For the salad

- 1 (14-ouncecan cannellini beans, drained and rinsed, or 1½ cups cooked
- 6 mushrooms, thinly sliced
- 1 zucchini, diced
- carrots, diced
- tablespoons fresh basil, chopped

Directions:

1. Make the dressing by whisking all the dressing ingredients together in a large bowl.
2. Toss all the salad ingredients with the dressing. For the best flavor, put the salad in a sealed container, shake it vigorously, and leave to marinate 15 to 30 minutes.

Macadamia-Cashew Patties

Preparation time: 10 minutes

Cooking time: 10 minutes

Servings: 4 patties

Ingredients:

- ¾ cup chopped macadamia nuts
- ¾ cup chopped cashews
- 1 medium carrot, grated
- 1 small onion, chopped
- 1 garlic clove, minced
- 1 jalapeño or other green chile, seeded and minced
- ¾ cup old-fashioned oats
- ¾ cup dry unseasoned bread crumbs
- 2 tablespoons minced fresh cilantro
- ½ teaspoon ground coriander
- Salt and freshly ground black pepper
- 2 teaspoons fresh lime juice

- Canola or grapeseed oil, for frying
- 4 sandwich rolls
- Lettuce leaves and condiment of choice

Directions:

1. In a food processor, combine the macadamia nuts, cashews, carrot, onion, garlic, chile, oats, bread crumbs, cilantro, coriander, and salt and pepper to taste. Process until well mixed. Add the lime juice and process until well blended. Taste, adjusting seasonings if necessary. Shape the mixture into 4 equal patties.
2. In a large skillet, heat a thin layer of oil over medium heat. Add the patties and cook until golden brown on both sides, turning once, about 10 minutes total. Serve on sandwich rolls with lettuce and condiments of choice.

Garlic Tahini Spread

Preparation time: 10 minutes

Cooking time: 15 minutes

Servings: 4

Nutritional Values (Per Serving):

- Calories 170
- Fat 7.3
- Fiber 4
- Carbs 1
- Protein 5

Ingredients:

- 1 cup coconut cream
- 2 tablespoons tahini paste
- 4 garlic cloves, minced
- Juice of 1 lime
- ¼ teaspoon turmeric powder
- A pinch of salt and black pepper
- 1 teaspoon sweet paprika
- 1 tablespoon olive oil

Directions:

1. Heat up a pan with the oil over medium heat, add the garlic, turmeric and paprika and cook for 5 minutes.
2. Add the rest of the ingredients, stir, cook over medium heat for 10 minutes more, blend using an immersion blender, divide into bowls and serve.

Balsamic Pearl Onions Bowls

Preparation time: 5 minutes

Cooking time: 15 minutes

Servings: 4

Nutritional Values (Per Serving):

- calories 120
- fat 2
- fiber 1
- carbs 2
- protein 2

Ingredients:

- 1 pound pearl onions, peeled
- A pinch of salt and black pepper
- 2 tablespoons avocado oil
- 4 tablespoons balsamic vinegar
- 1 tablespoon chives, chopped

Directions:

1. Heat up a pan with the oil over medium heat, add the pearl onions, salt, pepper and the other ingredients, cook for 15 minutes, divide into bowls and serve as a snack.

Basil Rice Bowls

Preparation time: 10 minutes

Cooking time: 20 minutes

Servings: 4

Nutritional Values (Per Serving):

- Calories 118
- Fat 11.5
- Fiber 2.2
- Carbs 5.9
- Protein 4

Ingredients:

- 2 cups cauliflower rice
- 1 cup veggie stock
- A pinch of salt and black pepper
- 1 teaspoon turmeric powder
- 1 teaspoon cumin, ground

- 1 teaspoon fennel seeds, crushed
- 2 tablespoons olive oil
- 2 tomatoes, cubed
- 1 cup black olives, pitted and sliced
- 1 bunch basil, chopped

Directions:

1. Heat up a pan with the oil over medium heat, add the cauliflower rice, stock, salt, pepper and the other ingredients, stir, cook for 20 minutes, divide into small bowls and serve as an appetizer.

Turmeric Peppers Platter

Preparation time: 10 minutes

Cooking time: 20 minutes

Servings: 4

Nutritional Values (Per Serving):

- Calories 120
- Fat 8.2
- Fiber 2
- Carbs 4
- Protein 2.3

Ingredients:

- 2 green bell peppers, cut into wedges
- 2 red bell peppers, cut into wedges
- 2 yellow bell peppers, cut into wedges
- 2 tablespoons avocado oil
- 2 garlic cloves, minced

- 1 bunch basil, chopped
- A pinch of salt and black pepper
- 2 tablespoons balsamic vinegar

Directions:

1. Heat up a pan with the oil over medium heat, add the garlic and the vinegar and cook for 2 minutes.
2. Add the peppers and the other ingredients, toss, cook over medium heat for 18 minutes, arrange them on a platter and serve as an appetizer.

Avocado and Strawberries Salad

Preparation time: 5 minutes

Cooking time: 0 minutes

Servings: 4

Nutritional Values (Per Serving):

- Calories 150
- Fat 3
- Fiber 3

- Carbs 5
- Protein 6

Ingredients:

- 2 avocados, pitted, peeled and cubed
- 1 cup strawberries, halved
- Juice of 1 lime
- 1 teaspoon almond extract
- 2 tablespoons almonds, chopped
- 1 tablespoon stevia

Directions:

1. In a bowl, combine the avocados with the strawberries, and the other ingredients, toss and serve.

Chocolate Watermelon Cups

Preparation time: 2 hours

Cooking time: 0 minutes

Servings: 4

Nutritional Values (Per Serving):

- Calories 164
- Fat 14.6
- Fiber 2.1
- Carbs 9.9
- Protein 2.1

Ingredients:

- 2 cups watermelon, peeled and cubed
- 1 tablespoon stevia
- 1 cup coconut cream
- 1 tablespoon cocoa powder
- 1 tablespoon mint, chopped

Directions:

1. In a blender, combine the watermelon with the stevia and the other ingredients, pulse well, divide into cups and keep in the fridge for 2 hours before serving.

Vanilla Raspberries Mix

Preparation time: 10 minutes

Cooking time: 10 minutes

Servings: 4

Nutritional Values (Per Serving):

- Calories 20
- Fat 0.4
- Fiber 2.1
- Carbs 4
- Protein 0.4

Ingredients:

- 1 cup water
- 1 cup raspberries
- 3 tablespoons stevia
- 1 teaspoon nutmeg, ground
- ½ teaspoon vanilla extract

Directions:

1. In a pan, combine the raspberries with the water and the other ingredients, toss, cook over medium heat for 10 minutes, divide into bowls and serve.

Ginger Cream

Preparation time: 10 minutes

Cooking time: 10 minutes

Servings: 4

Nutritional Values (Per Serving):

- Calories 280
- Fat 28.6
- Fiber 2.7
- Carbs 7
- Protein 2.8

Ingredients:

- 2 tablespoons stevia
- 2 cups coconut cream
- 1 teaspoon vanilla extract
- 1 tablespoon cinnamon powder
- ¼ tablespoon ginger, grated

Directions:

1. In a pan, combine the cream with the stevia and other ingredients, stir, cook over medium heat for 10 minutes, divide into bowls and serve cold.

Chocolate Ginger Cookies

Preparation time: 10 minutes

Cooking time: 20 minutes

Servings: 6

Nutritional Values (Per Serving):

- Calories 252
- Fat 41.6
- Fiber 6.5
- Carbs 11.7
- Protein 3

Ingredients:

- 2 cups almonds, chopped
- 2 tablespoons flaxseed mixed with 3 tablespoons water
- ¼ cup avocado oil
- 2 tablespoons stevia

- ¼ cup cocoa powder
- 1 teaspoon baking soda

Directions:

1. In your food processor, combine the almonds with the flaxseed mix and the other ingredients, pulse well, scoop tablespoons out of this mix, arrange them on a lined baking sheet, flatten them a bit and cook at 360 degrees F for 20 minutes.
2. Serve the cookies cold.

Coconut Salad

Preparation time: 10 minutes

Cooking time: 0 minutes

Servings: 6

Nutritional Values (Per Serving):

- Calories 250
- Fat 23.8
- Fiber 5.8
- Carbs 8.9
- Protein 4.5

Ingredients:

- 2 cups coconut flesh, unsweetened and shredded
- ½ cup walnuts, chopped
- 1 cup blackberries

- 1 tablespoon stevia
- 1 tablespoon coconut oil, melted

Directions:

1. In a bowl, combine the coconut with the walnuts and the other ingredients, toss and serve.

Mint Cookies

Preparation time: 10 minutes

Cooking time: 20 minutes

Servings: 6

Nutritional Values (Per Serving):

- Calories 190
- Fat 7.32
- Fiber 2.2
- Carbs 4
- Protein 3

Ingredients:

- 2 cups coconut flour
- 3 tablespoons flaxseed mixed with
- 4 tablespoons water
- ½ cup coconut cream
- ½ cup coconut oil, melted

- 3 tablespoons stevia
- 2 teaspoons mint, dried
- 2 teaspoons baking soda

Directions:

1. In a bowl, mix the coconut flour with the flaxseed, coconut cream and the other ingredients, and whisk really well.
2. Shape balls out of this mix, place them on a lined baking sheet, flatten them, introduce in the oven at 370 degrees F and bake for 20 minutes.
3. Serve the cookies cold.

Mint Avocado Bars

Preparation time: 10 minutes

Cooking time: 25 minutes

Servings: 6

Nutritional Values (Per Serving):

- Calories 230
- Fat 12.2
- Fiber 4.2
- Carbs 15.4
- Protein 5.8

Ingredients:

- 1 teaspoon almond extract
- ½ cup coconut oil, melted
- 2 tablespoons stevia
- 1 avocado, peeled, pitted and mashed

- 2 cups coconut flour
- 1 tablespoon cocoa powder

Directions:

1. In a bowl, combine the coconut oil with the almond extract, stevia and the other ingredients and whisk well.
2. Transfer this to baking pan, spread evenly, introduce in the oven and cook at 370 degrees F and bake for 25 minutes.
3. Cool down, cut into bars and serve.

Nut Fudge

Preparation time: 8 minutes

Cooking time: 1.5 hours

Servings: 3

Nutritions:

- Calories 144
- Fat 13
- Fiber 2.4
- Carbs 9.5
- Protein 5

Ingredients:

- 1 tablespoon almonds, crushed
- 4 tablespoon almond butter

- ½ teaspoon vanilla extract
- 1 tablespoon Erythritol

Directions:

1. Take the mixing bowl and combine in it the almond butter, vanilla extract, and Erythritol.
2. Transfer the bowl on the water bath, start to preheat it, and stir gently.
3. When the mixture is homogenous – add crushed almonds, stir it, and remove from the water bath.
4. Place the butter mixture in the mini muffin molds and transfer in the freezer.
5. Freeze it for 1.5 hours.

Mug Cake

Preparation time: 8 minutes

Cooking time: 1.5 hours

Servings: 4

Nutritions:

- Calories 91
- Fat 8.3
- Fiber 1.8
- Carbs 3.8
- Protein 2.1

Ingredients:

- 4 tablespoons pecans, chopped
- 4 teaspoon of cocoa powder
- 4 tablespoon almond flour
- 1 teaspoon vanilla extract
- ½ teaspoon baking powder

- 4 tablespoon almond milk
- 4 teaspoon Erythritol

Directions:

1. In the mixing bowl mix up together cocoa powder, almond flour, vanilla extract, baking powder, almond milk, and Erythritol.
2. When the mixture is smooth – add chopped pecans. Stir it. Transfer the batter in the mugs and place in the oven.
3. Cook the mug cakes for 10 minutes on 360F. Eat the cakes directly from the mugs.

Cocoa Ice Cream

Preparation time: 10 minutes

Cooking time: 30 minutes

Servings: 2

Nutritions:

- Calories 281
- Fat 28.7
- Fiber 2.9
- Carbs 7.3
- Protein 2.9

Ingredients:

- 1 can coconut milk
- 1 teaspoon of cocoa powder
- 1 tablespoon Erythritol
- ½ teaspoon vanilla extract

Directions:

1. Mix up together the coconut milk, cocoa powder, and Erythritol.
2. Add vanilla extract and stir until smooth.
3. Place the coconut mixture in the ice cube molds and place in the freezer for 30 minutes.
4. Then transfer the frozen coconut milk mixture in the blender and blend until smooth.
5. When you get smooth and solid ice cream mixture – it is cooked.

Almond Fat Bombs

Preparation time: 10 minutes

Cooking time: 25 minutes

Servings: 7

Nutritions:

- Calories 156
- Fat 13.2
- Fiber 3.3
- Carbs 10
- Protein 4.2

Ingredients:

- 1 cup almond flour
- 2 tablespoon Erythritol
- 1 teaspoon vanilla extract
- ¼ cup coconut butter
- 1 tablespoon almonds, crushed

Directions:

1. In the mixing bowl combine together almond flour and crushed almonds.
2. Add Erythritol, vanilla extract, and coconut butter.
3. Use the fork and knead the smooth and soft dough. Add more coconut butter if desired.
4. After this, make the medium size balls with the help of the fingertips and place them in the fridge for at least 25 minutes.
5. When the fat bombs are solid – they are cooked. Store the dessert in the fridge up to 5 days.

Brownies

Preparation time: 10 minutes

Cooking time: 15 minutes

Servings: 16

Nutritions:

- Calories 100
- Fat 7.8
- Fiber 2
- Carbs 10protein 3.7

Ingredients:

- 1 cup almond milk yogurt
- ½ teaspoon baking powder
- 4 tablespoon cocoa powder
- 1 teaspoon vanilla extract
- 2 cups almond flour
- ½ cup Erythritol

- ¾ teaspoon salt
- 1 tablespoon flax meal

Directions:

1. Preheat the oven to 355F.
2. In the mixing bowl combine together all the dry ingredients.
3. Then add almond milk yogurt and stir the mixture until you get the batter.
4. Line the tray with the baking paper and transfer batter on it.
5. Flatten brownie batter with the help of a spatula.
6. Place the brownie in the preheated oven and cook for 15 minutes.
7. Then remove the tray with a brownie from the oven.
8. Cut the brownie into 16 serving bars.
9. Transfer the brownie bars in the fridge for 6 hours.

Roasted Squash

Preparation time: 10 minutes

Cooking time: 1 hour

Servings: 3

Nutritions:

- Calories 182
- Fat 15 G
- Carbohydrates 12.3 G
- Sugar 11 G
- Protein 3.2 G
- Cholesterol 0 Mg

Ingredients:

- 2 lbs. summer squash, cut into 1-inch pieces
- 1/8 tsp pepper
- 1/8 tsp garlic powder
- 3 tbsp olive oil

- 1 large lemon juice
- 1/8 tsp paprika
- Pepper
- Salt

Directions:

1. Preheat the oven to 400 F/ 204 C. Spray a baking tray with cooking spray.
2. Place squash pieces onto the prepared baking tray and drizzle with olive oil. Season with paprika, pepper, and garlic powder.
3. Squeeze lemon juice over the squash and bake in preheated oven for 50-60 minutes. Serve hot and enjoy.